Little Explorers Guide to
VICTORIAN
NATIONAL PARKS

Outdoor activities and experiences for adventurous kids

Written by CHLOE BUTTERFIELD

Illustrated by DEBORAH BIANCHETTO

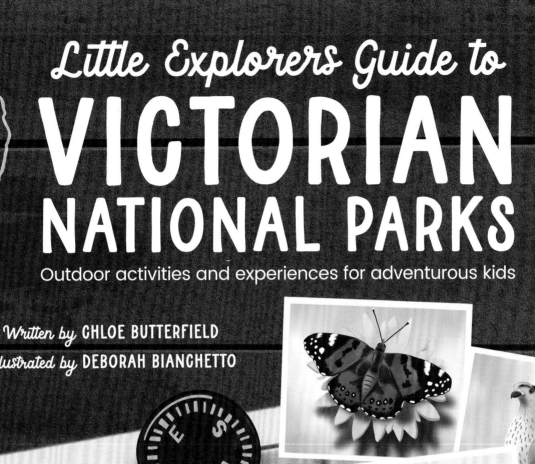

TABLE OF CONTENTS

Mildura

Wangaratta

Shepparton

Bendigo

Hamilton

Melbourne

Geelong

CROAJINGOLONG
NATIONAL PARK

Far away from the hustle and bustle of cities, water laps at your canoe and birds twitter overhead as you soak in the view of the vast and endless sea. This watery wonderland is fantastic for adventurers, with secret inlets to explore, wildlife around every corner and special treats for keen birdwatchers. Find new energy for new passions at Croajingolong.

CROAJINGOLONG NATIONAL PARK
ID CARD

PARK ESTABLISHED: 1979
KNOWN FOR: INCREDIBLE DIVERSITY OF PLANTS AND ANIMALS
SIZE: 875KM²
MEETING PLACE OF: BIDAWAL AND NINDI-NGUDJAM NGARIGU MONERO PEOPLE
GEOGRAPHY: PRISTINE WATERWAYS REACHING INTO DENSE FOREST AND ENORMOUS DUNES

LITTLE EXPLORER'S GUIDE

LITTLE TERN

These little wings fly thousands of kilometres across the world to be here with you, from east Asia to Australia and back again. When they arrive, in their tiny black caps, they're incredibly tired – so watch from a distance, explorers.

Did you know that Little Terns make their nests on the ground? They scrape a shallow hole in the sand and fill it with goodies such as shells and seaweed. You'll know it's time for laying eggs when their legs change colour from black to yellow.

TREE FROGS

Thanks to the low, wet areas and healthy vegetation here, you're standing in frog paradise. There are so many different types of frogs here that your evenings will be filled with frog song. Some of the special **amphibians** that live here include Peron's, Blue Mountains, Lesueur's, Green and Brown Tree Frogs and even froglets! Take a wander at night for your best chance to spot them and download a frog app to help you identify their calls.

TIGER SNAKE

Thick with a short head, Tiger Snakes don't always have stripes. Depending on where they live, their colour can vary from black to grey to sandy or striped. During winter these shy reptiles keep warm by sleeping in burrows that other animals have made, and with real estate at a premium sometimes there can be more than 20 in one place.

Even though Tiger Snakes are dangerously **venomous**, they still use constriction (squeezing) before eating their **prey** – fascinating behaviour.

SCARLET HONEYEATER

Just as the name suggests, this beautiful bird flits around the bush with a curvy beak used for reaching all the sweet treats such as nectar and fruit. Males are bright red and females plain brown. These nomads move around throughout the year, following gum trees in bloom. Listen out for their *swit-sweet-switty-switty-switty* chirps.

GREY-HEADED FLYING-FOX

Don't forget to look up – you might just spot big groups of bats **roosting** by day and flying out at dusk. Families live together and mums hang by their feet and catch babies in their wings as they are born!

Sneak up quietly as you watch – these **nocturnal** beauties need rest during the day to allow for big flights of up to 50 kilometres in a night seeking food and, in the process, **pollinating** our forests and mangroves. Flying-foxes are sensitive to heat, so you'll always find them near fresh water, where they can drink and stay cool.

FUNNEL-WEB SPIDERS

Beneath your feet, under rocks, logs and rotting timber, big chunky spiders with four spinnerets wait ever so patiently for their traps to go off. At the door of their burrows they build special webs with trip lines. When a small animal stumbles across a line, the spider feels the movement and runs out to attack! When it's time to grow up and find a partner, males leave their burrows and go on a long wander, sniffing out female pheromones.

TOPKNOT PIGEON

Looking windswept and fabulous, with the coolest 'hairstyle' in the canopy, these birds are bigger than your average street pigeon. They love hanging upside-down to reach fruit – in fact they like fruit so much that we call them **frugivores**. Even the babies eat fruit, but it gets delivered to them a little differently – regurgitated by their parents and it is sometimes called 'pigeon milk'.

MAINLAND DUSKY ANTECHINUS

We're still learning about these **carnivorous marsupials** and scientists recently discovered that they can climb trees! Usually crazy dirt diggers, they fossick for insects, worms and spiders using long claws for scratching and long whiskers for sensing. In winter they make long burrows filled with grass, then breed. It's so intense that the males don't even eat and become so exhausted that they die soon after.

WONDERFUL WHALES

With a mighty push, whales surge up from the depths, revealing their enormous bodies as they splash back down in a spectacular fashion. We don't exactly know why they jump – it could just be for fun!

Many whales **migrate** up and down the coastline, travelling long distances to warm water to have their babies and back down again with their newborns to find food. We are still learning everyday about these incredible journeys. Luckily whale hunting was banned in 1985, so there are more of these amazing creatures for us to enjoy today.

ACTIVITIES

SYMMETRY SKETCH

Funnel-web spiders are beautiful, symmetrical creatures.

Draw the other half of this fascinating animal using the grid to guide you.

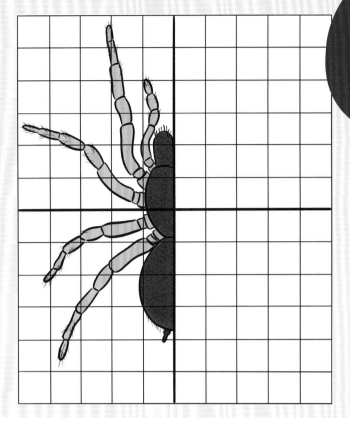

RANGER'S TIP

Creepy crawlies may make you shudder, but it's our job to look after one another. Spiders, insects and arthropods are an important part of the balance of this ecosystem. Show them your respect by observing from a distance and being careful not to disturb their homes.

I.D. ME

Can you tell who is who in the wetlands? Read the notes below and draw a line to the frog that matches each description.

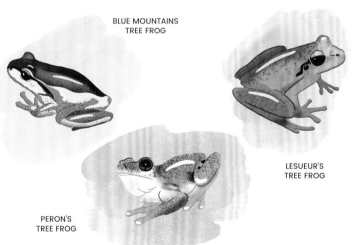

BLUE MOUNTAINS TREE FROG

LESUEUR'S TREE FROG

PERON'S TREE FROG

FROG 1

- Grey or light brown back
- Tiny green spots
- Cross-shaped pupil on eye

FROG 2

- Brown back and green sides
- Dark brown stripe from nose to arm
- Bright red inner legs

FROG 3

- Pale brown
- Black stripe that passes through the eye
- Black or purple patches on the back of the thigh

BENEATH THE SURFACE

BUILD A BATHYSCOPE TO HELP YOU LOOK UNDERWATER. USE MATERIALS FROM YOUR RECYCLING BIN OR CAMPSITE WITH PERMISSION FROM YOUR ADULTS. WHICH WATERY WORLDS WILL YOU DISCOVER BENEATH THE SURFACE?

WILSONS PROMONTORY
NATIONAL PARK

Home to Aboriginal communities for at least 6,500 years,
where rivers meet the ocean and golden light kisses the
soft colours of the landscape; you won't believe you've
found this much quiet so close to the city.
Here you're as far south as you can travel in the state, at
the edge of Victoria's biggest marine park. There are so
many beaches, you might just get one all to yourself.

WILSONS PROMONTORY NATIONAL PARK
ID CARD

PARK ESTABLISHED: 1898
KNOWN FOR: VAST OCEAN AND CURIOUS CREATURES
SIZE: 500km²
HOME OF: GUNAIKURNAI AND BOONWURRUNG PEOPLE
GEOGRAPHY: GRANITE MOUNTAIN CHAIN SURROUNDED BY PRISTINE BEACHES

LITTLE EXPLORER'S GUIDE

VICTORIAN SMOOTH FROGLET

Waaaaaaark - pip - pip - pip - pip: it's a froglet calling to its mates. With a smooth white belly, adorned with brown spots and a yellow throat for the males, these **amphibians** are unmistakable. Unlike many frogs, they lay their eggs on land and the babies wait patiently until the ground becomes flooded to hatch.

AUSTRALIAN FUR SEAL

On the islands just off this coastline, breeding groups of seals called 'colonies' stake their claim to the warm rocks where they have their pups each summer. They have to be fast and clever, because much bigger predators such as sharks lurk in their feeding grounds, hungry for a meal. They move lightning fast in the water, diving down to 200 metres to catch fish, squid and octopus.

Fur seals are special because of their double layer of fur and small wiggly ears on the outside, while males have dark hair around their neck like a lion's mane. Look out for these features.

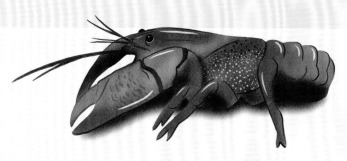

SOUTH GIPPSLAND SPINY CRAYFISH

In freshwater only, blue spines with sharp white tips peek out from hidden burrows under rocks and tree roots. Crayfish eat all manner of things, including plants, **invertebrates**, fungi and bacteria, keeping waterways healthy and clear. They wear a hard 'carapace' for a back, like a knight in a suit of armour and mum crayfish sometimes hide a secret: babies hatched underneath her tail that hitch a ride for some months after birth – how mysterious!

WEEDY SEADRAGON

These dragons of the deep float along on the current, dangling their body parts like seaweed for **camouflage**. At night, the ladies and gentlemen dance to show they like each other and not long after, eggs are laid. Seadragon dads carry the eggs and can haul up to 250 under their tail.

GREAT WHITE SHARK

Arguably the most famous fish in the world, Great Whites are an important part of this marine park's food chain. After existing for 250 million years and surviving five **extinction** events, we think they've truly earned their place. Shark pups use this area as a nursery to keep them safe as they grow and learn the ways of the ocean.

Great Whites are excellent at finding prey because they have a special 'olfactory bulb' for smelling – it is bigger than that of any other shark and can feel electrical currents through the water, which they use to draw themselves a mental 'map' of the ocean.

SOOTY OYSTERCATCHER

Tiptoe, tiptoe, stab! An oystercatcher pierces its **prey** with its pointy beak like a fork. As black as soot from a chimney, their striking feathers are easy to spot. Sooties won't settle for anything less than an ocean view, never venturing further than about 50 metres from the beach. They're so attached to the ocean that they even drink seawater… they have special salt glands next to their eyes that take salt out of their blood and eject it from their bodies – talk about adaptations!

NEW HOLLAND MOUSE

An endangered friend of the bush and sadly **extinct** in most places in Victoria, the New Holland Mouse lives here behind the protection of a special 'exclusion fence' to keep **predators** out. These mice like to live in places with soft, sandy soil because their favourite thing to do is burrow! Although they might look a bit like a common House Mouse, they have bigger eyes for living their best **nocturnal** lifestyle – larger eyes let in more light so they can find tasty treats such as seeds in the dark.

EMU

Few animals wander through the bush as majestically as Emus. These huge flightless birds make grunting, drumming and booming sounds. They're omnivorous and like to feast on seeds, fruits, insects and plants. The Emu here are important for spreading the seeds of native plants through their **scats.**

MOUNTAIN ASH

Soaring to 90 metres high and more than seven metres wide, this is the tallest flowering plant in the world! Mountain Ash don't have as many fancy adaptations as other plants, so they have to grow super fast and get strong quickly. After fire, tiny seeds plunge to the ground and regrow soon after. When fire burns only one side of the tree, it hollows out a section perfect for use as shelter for the traditional owners of this land for many thousands of years.

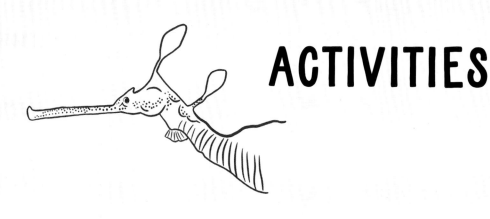

ACTIVITIES

MISSING PIECES

Some of the weedy sea dragon is missing! Use wiggly lines and camouflage colours to draw the rest of its strange floating body.

RANGER'S TIP

Lookout for whales splashing around in Norman Bay during migration season.

"The Prom has been a special place for people for thousands of years. There is something very powerful about this park, it's wild and untamed and runs its own weather system most of the time."
Ranger Lucy

WHO AM I?

Design your own clues for a 'guess the animal' game. You might like to use some facts from this chapter.

CLUE 1

CLUE 2

CLUE 3

SURPRISE, MY ANIMAL IS A

TOOTHY GRIN

BUILD A BIG MOUTH WITH MANY TEETH LIKE A GREAT WHITE SHARK USING MATERIALS YOU CAN FIND IN YOUR RECYCLING BIN. IT'S FUN TO REPURPOSE ITEMS THAT WOULD OTHERWISE BECOME WASTE.

FRENCH ISLAND
NATIONAL PARK

This very special destination offers up two protected parks at the same time – a national park on land and a marine park underwater. Together they offer a safe place for rare and endangered animals that have been brought here for protection and they live among the many ecosystems here for you to discover.

From wetlands to mangroves, saltmarshes, forest and the beaches that first greet you, there is something here for everyone. Ride or walk around your favourite parts and spot more Koalas than you will believe possible as you soak it all in.

FRENCH ISLAND NATIONAL PARK
ID CARD

PARK ESTABLISHED: 1997
KNOWN FOR: HEALTHY KOALAS AND WILDLIFE, SAFE FROM FOXES AND DISEASE
SIZE: 111km² OF NATIONAL PARK AND 28km² OF MARINE PARK
HOME OF: BUNURONG PEOPLE
GEOGRAPHY: ROCKY BEACHES AND WETLANDS FRINGE QUIET, OPEN SPACES RICH WITH DIVERSITY

LITTLE EXPLORER'S GUIDE

NATIVE ORCHIDS

More than 100 types of orchids live here and many of them look completely different to one another. Orchids have six petals and rely on a special type of fungus to be able to **germinate**. Take the walking track along the old coast road to see the special French Island Spider Orchid and see how many others you can spot growing on the ground or wrapped around trees. Never pick orchids – they are protected under Australian law.

LITTLE PENGUIN

The little pink feet, blue-black feathers and waddle of the smallest penguin in the world combine to melt hearts year after year. Unlike other penguins, they don't love ice, so hang out here among the roc and sand.

Ever wondered why they waddle? They have little legs but big feet for swimming (like wearing fins for snorkelling). Penguins eat lots o important foods like fish, squid, krill and **crustaceans**, so any chang to the penguins gives scientists a clue that there might be somethi wrong in the food chain.

WETLANDS

The wetlands here are so special to animals *all around the world* that they are listed as a protected **RAMSAR** site. Wetlands keep our waterways, **habitats**, plants, animals AND humans safe and healthy by slowing down the water that runs off the land, 'holding' it and allowing **sediment**, pollutants and rubbish to sink to the bottom and become trapped, before the clear water runs out to the ocean. They protect the land from big storms using mangrove trees and their strong roots as a buffer to soften the impact. As if wetlands weren't amazing enough already, did you know that they trap about 35 per cent of Earth's carbon?

SALTMARSH

Under the soil secret magic is happening – tiny microbes are breaking down and recycling plant matter. The saltmarsh here is unusually large and incredibly important as we fight rising sea levels.

The saltmarsh collects **sediment** that washes onto its shores and builds up the height of the land which holds back the sea as it rises. Saltmarsh also provides amazing **habitat**, protection against storms AND traps carbon so that it can't escape out into the atmosphere.

WEDGE-TAILED EAGLE

High in the sky with a tail in the shape of a wedge and circling in search of lunch, Australia's largest bird of **prey** can be seen, giving a steely stare as it drifts by. These birds are enormous – they can weigh more than five kilograms and have a wingspan of over two metres. Wedge-taileds are exceptional hunters because they can actually squeeze and lengthen their eyeballs to zoom their vision, a bit like a camera lens.

EASTERN CURLEW

Just one of the many migratory species found here, this critically endangered bird lives half the year in its breeding grounds in Russia and China, then flies across the world to spend summer with us. It uses the stars and Earth's magnetic field to navigate and travels 30,000 kilometres in a year, flapping the whole time as it can't glide – phenomenal!

When the birds arrive they're very tired and very hungry, so watch from a distance and let them rest. Eastern Curlews can live to 20 years old, and if they do will have flown the equivalent distance from the Earth to the *moon* in their lifetime.

EASTERN BARRED BANDICOOT

Ecologists released these bandicoots here to provide them with a safe home away from foxes and humans as they were almost **extinct** in Victoria. They use special cameras to watch how they're doing and see them running and hiding in the tall grass and digging pits in loose soil looking for a yummy snack of plant bulbs, **invertebrates** and fruits.

CREEPING CRUSTACEANS

Many creatures live here under the sand, including ghost crabs – the super fast racers that dress in white for **camouflage** and hide in sandy burrows. Take a night walk to see if you can spot them. Can you see one claw that's bigger than the other? They use their claws to communicate by hitting them against the ground or rubbing them together to make a sound.

KOALA

Look up, explorers, because this place has the most significant population of Koala in Victoria and a whole forest of them are cuddled up atop the canopy. You'll find them sleeping 20 hours a day nestled in the forks of eucalypts – the only food they like to eat.

Koala babies live in backwards-facing pouches when small, then hitch a ride on mum's back. As they get older they eat liquid poo called 'pap' to help them get used to the strong taste of gum leaves. Switch on all your senses for koala clues – look for deep scratch-marks on trees, avocado-shaped droppings, low grunting calls or the smell of eucalyptus.

ACTIVITIES

"French Island is a really unique and diverse park. There are so many wild and natural landscapes here. There are no foxes, possums or kangaroos on French Island, so we have a lot of wild life that's different to what you usually see on the mainland."
Ranger Rach

CLASSIFICATION STATION

Scientists classify animals and plants into groups by finding things about them that are similar. Decide three different ways to group these animals and draw a picture of them in the correct circles.

KOALA
EASTERN BARRED BANDICOOT
EASTERN CURLEW
WEDGE-TAILED EAGLE
LITTLE PENGUIN
CRUSTACEAN

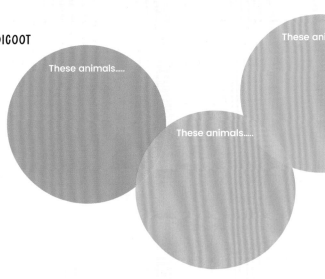

These animals.....

These animals.....

These animals.....

RANGER'S TIP

Keep the animals and plants safe from disease and pests by cleaning your boots before you set foot on the island.

CODE CRACKER

Solve the hidden message using the code below.

A	B	C	D	E	F	G	H	I	J	K	L	M

N	O	P	Q	R	S	T	U	V	W	X	Y	Z

_____

_____

PENGUIN WALKIE TALKIE

PENGUINS WADDLE BECAUSE OF THEIR SHORT LEGS AND BIG FEET. MAKE UP YOUR OWN PENGUIN WALK AND LANGUAGE JUST FOR FUN.

KiNGLAKE
NATIONAL PARK

So close to Melbourne, this section of the Great Dividing Range demonstrates the true resilience of the Australian bush; growing back strong and thick after bushfires some years ago. This park represents new life and opportunities.

Breathe in the smell of eucalyptus as you follow gently winding rivers and tumbling waterfalls, spotting moss and lichen among the rocks and listening to birds chirping overhead. Pack a picnic and prepare for some of the best views in Victoria.

KINGLAKE NATIONAL PARK

ID CARD

PARK ESTABLISHED: 1928
KNOWN FOR: PICNICS WITH SPECTACULAR VIEWS
SIZE: 216KM²
HOME OF: TAUNGURUNG AND WURUNDJERI PEOPLES
GEOGRAPHY: ICONIC BUSH STRADDLING THE SLOPES OF THE GREAT DIVIDING RANGE

LITTLE EXPLORER'S GUIDE

POWERFUL OWL

Peering through the darkness glow yellow eyes, atop a tall body, feathered legs and powerful, sharp talons. This is the largest owl in the country and is often found near waterways. They mate for life and favour their own special territory. Listen for a low *woo-hoo* in the treetops at night because these owls live in small family groups and hunt for midnight treats of possums, gliders and birds.

PLATYPUS

As you peer into the dark, cool water, past your own reflection, watch carefully for bubbles floating to the surface. Platypus use special sensors in their bills to track the electrical signals of their **prey** underwater. They use their bills to forage and sift for **invertebrates** at the bottom, which makes the bubbles you can see. Then they stash the food in their cheeks to grind up later.

These monotremes are **mammals**, but they lay two eggs and are so weird that they were thought to be a joke when first discovered by Europeans. Platypus don't have pouches, so the mums curl up with the eggs to keep them warm in long burrows in the banks of the river.

PINK ROBIN

You'll need your keenest senses in thick bush to spot a 'pinky'. Look for black and pink feathers on cute, round bodies and listen for a *chwit-tr-tr-tr*. You might even be able to spot one of their plush comfy nests, made from squishy moss and tangled together with spider webs and soft leaves – look for them perched dramatically on the ends of branches.

MOUNTAIN GREY GUM

Growing to 65 metres tall, these old gums watch over the landscape. Just imagine the things they've seen! When it's time for their bark to shed it peels off in beautiful long ribbons. When it's time to bloom, bees absolutely love their little white flowers, which are full of nectar.

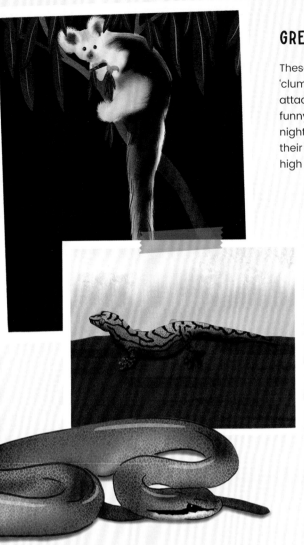

GREATER GLIDER

These big guys look like teddy bears and are sometimes called the 'clumsy cousins' as their skin membrane which allows them to glide is attached to their elbow, not their wrist. This makes it trickier to land, but funny to watch. They sleep in hollows during the day and are active at night, travelling up to 100 metres in a single glide, marking trees with their scent as they go. Explore with a torch at night and look way up high to get a lucky glimpse.

MARBLED GECKO

Sticky feet like velcro make these lizards perfectly designed for arboreal life. They hide under the bark and their beautiful marbled skin perfectly matches the trees' shades of brown, making for excellent **camouflage**. Take a night walk to watch them feed on the insects attracted to the lights of your campground. Look closely to spot the hidden orange specks on their tails.

TREE FERNS

Since dinosaurs roamed, tree ferns have been an important part of the landscape. In 2009, much of this park was burned by fire, but tree ferns protected themselves with thick bark. These special plants give shade to the ground, which keeps it moist and allows beneficial critters to live underground. **Marsupials** eat these critters and **prey** animals eat marsupials, so tree ferns are literal building blocks for healthy **ecosystems**.

WHITE-LIPPED SNAKE

These lovely specimens are named after the white stripe that lashes across their face, lining where their lips would be (if they had any). They're nicely adapted to the cool weather here because they're small, so can heat up faster than big snakes, and eggs don't need to be kept warm because they don't lay any!

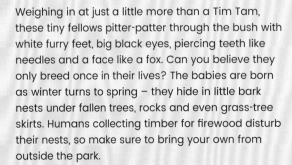

PEREGRINE FALCON

Diving from the sky at more than 300 kilometres per hour – the speed of a bullet train – this is the world's fastest animal! Watch them fly high to search for **prey**, then almost fall out of the air with magnificent speed as they descend upon a meal. Sometimes pairs even help each other to hunt – dad scares a flock of birds and mum dives in to catch one. What teamwork!

WHITE-FOOTED DUNNART

Weighing in at just a little more than a Tim Tam, these tiny fellows pitter-patter through the bush with white furry feet, big black eyes, piercing teeth like needles and a face like a fox. Can you believe they only breed once in their lives? The babies are born as winter turns to spring – they hide in little bark nests under fallen trees, rocks and even grass-tree skirts. Humans collecting timber for firewood disturb their nests, so make sure to bring your own from outside the park.

ACTIVITIES

NEW SPECIES ALERT!

Invent your own new creature by combining the top and bottom of two that live here. Which special skills will it have and what will its name be?

RANGER'S TIP

Don't forget to bring your own wood and always check the fire danger rating to see when it's safe to light a campfire.

HOME AMONG THE GUM TREES

Draw all the animals that you think benefit from Mountain Grey Gums. You can draw them on the tree, in the tree or under the tree, depending on where they spend most of their time.

NO PEEKING

PLATYPUS USE ELECTRO SENSING (NOT SIGHT) TO FIND FOOD UNDERWATER. WORK WITH A FRIEND TO TAKE TURNS BEING BLINDFOLDED AND FIND YOUR WAY AROUND YOUR CAMPSITE WITH YOUR PARTNER GIVING YOU DIRECTIONS. FIND OUT HOW TRICKY IT IS WHEN YOU CAN'T RELY ON SIGHT! DON'T FORGET TO ASK YOUR ADULTS' PERMISSION FIRST.

Great Otway
NATIONAL PARK

Hidden secrets line the Great Ocean Road, where quiet animals hide in the safety of cool forest and cutaway cliffs host surfers who rip along pumping beasts of waves. Home to the tallest treetop walk in the world and a sweep of dinosaur fossil discoveries and waterfalls nestled into the earth, Great Otway holds so many treasures.

GREAT OTWAY NATIONAL PARK
ID CARD

PARK ESTABLISHED: 1981
KNOWN FOR: TALL FORESTS AND OCEAN CLIFFS
SIZE: 1,000KM²
HOME OF: GADUBANUD PEOPLE
GEOGRAPHY: RICH FOREST ATOP SEDIMENTARY ROCK

LITTLE EXPLORER'S GUIDE

SOUTHERN BOOBOOK

The smallest of all our owls, boobook are a delight to spot. Their yellowy-green eyes are a mesmerising contrast to their immaculate chocolate feathers. Boobooks are **nocturnal** and hunt at night – the bush is a smorgasbord of delights for their wide range of tastes and they can even catch insects and bats in mid air! You guessed it, they call *boo-book* in the darkness, which is how they got their name.

GLOW WORMS

Like something from a dream, glow worms light up caves and rocky overhangs throughout the forest, turning it into a magical, twinkling extravaganza. These 'worms' are actually the **larvae** of ancient flies. They spend nine months in this form, living inside a sticky mucus tube and hanging off threads from the roof.

At night, a chemical reaction happens inside their bodies and causes them to switch on their 'lights'. They mesmerise their **prey** with their twinkling, then trap them in the sticky lines and eat them up for dinner.

RED-NECKED WALLABY

You're sure to spot many of these macropod friends on your visit. They are grey with a red-coloured patch around their necks. The adults feed in open grassy areas. Babies however, once they're out of the pouch, get 'hidden' in nearby bushes for safety. Watch out for **scats** that are smooth and greeny-yellow.

EASTERN BLUE-TONGUE

This giant skink grows to 60 centimetres long and sports a grumpy face as it lumbers along, looking for **arthropods** to crush with its strong jaws. They use their scale colours for **camouflage** against fallen leaves. If alarmed, they move towards the threat and poke out their tongue. This may look funny to us, but bright blue inside a pink mouth is a warning to **predators**. If more gusto is needed, they'll hiss, bite and drop their tails to get away – they can grow a new tail later!

LONG-NOSED POTOROO

Pottering along, night after night, potoroo help our forests to grow by feeding on fungi and spreading **spores** in their **scats**. The spores grow into new fungi which help trees to take up more water and nutrients so they can grow tall.

The plants thank the potoroos by providing safe homes for them to shelter in and fallen leaves which they use for restful day naps. Look near stringybark and wet areas for small holes in the ground – these are evidence of potoroo pottering.

EASTERN YELLOW ROBIN

Flashes of gold light up the foliage as robins collect bark, grass and plants to make nests that they stick together with spider webs. So nothing is wasted, they eat the spiders while they're at it! Listen for their *peep-peep-peep* early in the morning.

REDWOODS

In 1936, a grove of redwoods was planted here as an experiment. Now at 60 metres tall and growing strong as ever, the redwoods are here to stay. This species can live to 2,000 years old and is the tallest tree in the world – one specimen in America holds the current record of 115 metres. Their rough, red-barked trunks make the best location for a game of hide-and-seek.

NANKEEN KESTREL

A small raptor with big abilities, the Nankeen Kestrel is a perfect specimen of aviation. When they spy **prey**, they can hover by flapping their wings super fast and using their fan-shaped tail to hold steady and change direction. They're the only bird of **prey** with this special skill. They have incredibly strong wings that won't bend in the wind and slots between their feathers make for a smoother ride as air flows through and causes less wind resistance – just like an aeroplane!

ACTIVITIES

WINNER WINNER, LIZARD DINNER

Go on a food walk and look closely for critters and plants. Draw on the dinner plate which ones a blue-tongue might like to eat. You might even like to write them a 'menu' for the day.

Lizard Dinner

KESTREL IN FLIGHT

Make a paper aeroplane and decorate it to look like a kestrel. Have a competition to see who flies the farthest. What modifications can you make to make yours even speedier?

RANGER'S TIP

While birds sing during the day and wallabies hop around, the real adventure comes out at night time, when the bush comes alive! Go out for a night-time bush walk and see what you can find.

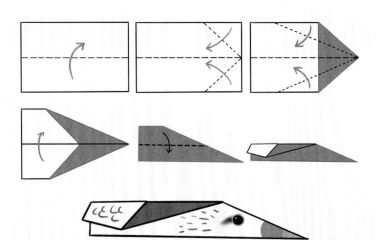

RADICAL REDWOODS
MEASURE A REDWOOD BY PACING OUT 60 METRES. DRAW THE LINE THAT SPANS THE LENGTH OF THE TREE AND THEN MEASURE YOURSELF AGAINST THE LINE... HOW MANY OF 'YOU' MAKE UP A TREE?

Lake Eildon
NATIONAL PARK

Lying stretched out and silent at the feet of the alps, the cool water of Lake Eildon laps gently at your toes as your body begins to sync to its gentle rhythm.

By day, explore your watery surroundings on watercraft or immerse yourself fully with a refreshing swim. By night, listen to the sounds of the bush as it comes alive all around you. Which secrets will you discover here?

LAKE EILDON NATIONAL PARK
ID CARD

PARK ESTABLISHED: 1997
KNOWN FOR: WATERSPORTS OF ALL TYPES
SIZE: 277KM²
HOME OF: TAUNGURUNG PEOPLE
GEOGRAPHY: FRESHWATER AS FAR AS THE EYE CAN SEE, SURROUNDED BY ACTIVE WILDLIFE

LITTLE EXPLORER'S GUIDE

BARKING OWL

In the forest, huge yellow eyes let in extra light for seeing clearly in the darkness. This is a very special place where Victoria's few remaining Barking Owls live, hunting at the edge of the forest and calling in all sorts of weird and wonderful ways. From sounds like a dog barking to a person screaming, these amazing birds certainly spice up the night.

EASTERN HORSESHOE BAT

A funny nose shaped like a horseshoe makes these tiny faces unmistakable. Bats use **echolocation** to 'see' where things are. The horseshoe shape of this nose helps to funnel the sound back to the bat's ears without the sound changing as it bounces off objects around them. When they're not being professional hunters, these guys like to hang upside-down in the abandoned mine shafts left here after the gold rush.

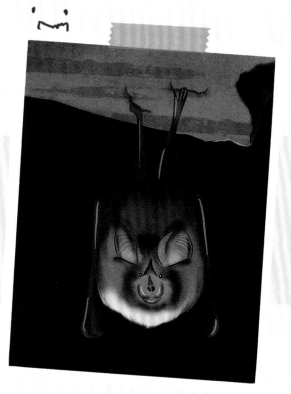

SPOTTED TREE FROG

Are you feeling lucky? Because that's exactly what you'll need to be in order to see these unusual endangered amphibians. Spotted Tree Frogs are fussy about their lifestyle; they like cool, clean water that runs fast and large boulders to hide around and lay their eggs under. Some are diurnal and some nocturnal depending on where they live – how strange! Look for their muted green, almost brown backs for amazing camouflage and fast mouths that snack on insects passing by.

AUSTRALIAN PELICAN

With a quick scooping action, pelicans open their wide pouched bills, capture their food and let the water run out, trapping delicious morsels inside. With a wriggle and flick, pelicans make sure their dinner is pointing down their throats before swallowing. Their bills are huge at almost 50 centimetres long, hold up to seven litres of water inside, and even have a tiny hook at the end for grabbing onto more slippery items. These expert eaters love teamwork, working together to push fish into shallow water, where scooping is simple.

MURRAY COD

Just below your toes in the slow-moving depths of Lake Eildon, huge fish weighing up to 100 kg or more glide effortlessly, searching for their next meal of birds, turtles, snakes or other fish. Cod dads are impeccable parents, looking after their eggs on the riverbed for around a month, constantly swimming back and forth, gently brushing their fins over the eggs to keep the clean water moving, and keeping watch for hungry predators.

BRUSH-TAILED PHASCOGALE

Bounding through the trees, rustles a furry little friend with a black bushy tail and pointy nose. Phascogales only eat meat and some of their favourites include insects and arachnids! Resting by day in hollows and fallen logs, these little guys pad their nests with all sorts of crazy things, such as tree bark, snake skins, hair, feathers and even dead animals. Look up at night to see them.

SWAMP WALLABY

Also known as Black Wallabies, these stocky, black-furred **marsupials** will eat at any time of day or night, chomping down grass, shrubs and ferns. They're not just found in swamps either – look for them anywhere the soil is moist and listen for them stamping their feet as they alert their pals to danger.

FERAL FOES

Nature is not always in perfect harmony in our national parks. More than 315 million birds and 595 million **reptiles** are killed by cats and foxes each year in Australia! There are many rare, small creatures that live here on the ground and happen to be rather delicious to these introduced **predators**. You can do your part by keeping cats indoors at all times and leaving dogs at home when you go out exploring our parks. Just the scent of a pet can deter native animals from returning to breed in an area.

ACTIVITIES

GO GO GRAPH

Lake Eildon is home to many incredible species of birds. Draw the type of bird you see in the space along the bottom and shade one square each time you see one. I wonder which bird you'll see the most of?

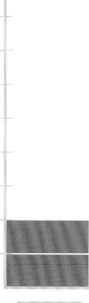

EYE SPY MATCH

The park comes alive at night with shining eyes, glimmering in the moonlight. Can you guess which eyes belong to which animal?

EASTERN HORSESHOE BAT

BARKING OWL

BLACK WALLABY

BRUSH—TAILED PHASCOGALE

RANGER'S TIP

Be sure to have an adult walk with you at night and remember to take a torch! Falling into water in the dark is not a risk you want to take.

NATURE ART
USE MATERIALS YOU CAN FIND IN NATURE (SUCH AS FALLEN LEAVES, STICKS, BARK OR ROCKS) AND ARRANGE THEM TO MAKE A PICTURE. DON'T FORGET TO PUT EVERYTHING BACK WHERE YOU FOUND IT WHEN YOU'RE FINISHED!

GRAMPIANS
NATIONAL PARK

High on sandstone cliffs, marvel at top-of-the-world views and breathe in crisp, clear air. The Grampians – also known as Gariwerd – may look magical, but the place also hides away special treasures such as ancient rock art and shelters linked to our unique Aboriginal heritage.

Here you'll find some of the best hikes in the country; so good, in fact, that people come from all over the world to walk them.

GRAMPIANS (GARIWERD) NATIONAL PARK
ID CARD

PARK ESTABLISHED: 1984
KNOWN FOR: MAGNIFICENT HIKING AND ROCK CLIMBING
SIZE: 1,688km²
MEETING PLACE OF: DJAB WURRUNG AND JARDWARDJALI PEOPLE
GEOGRAPHY: SANDSTONE RIDGES AND DEEP GORGES

LITTLE EXPLORER'S GUIDE

RED-TAILED BLACK-COCKATOO

Waddling along and squawking with a *kreeeee*, Red-taileds chomp down on seeds, stopping occasionally to preen themselves with a special oil patch on their backs. These big birds enjoy a long sleep in and won't begin feeding until the weather is warm. They have 'zygodactyl' feet with two toes pointing forwards and two pointing backwards – maybe this is why they always enter their hollows tail-first.

GALAH

Noisy screechers by day and snuggled up to **roost** in enormous numbers by night, pink-and-grey Galah are cheeky little fellows. You might even hear an Aussie call someone a 'Galah' to match the silliness of this feathered friend. Galah meet a partner and stay together for life. You can tell them apart by looking out for brown eyes on males and red eyes for females.

COPPERHEAD SNAKE

Muscly, scaly bodies slither through the undergrowth looking for their next meal of **ectothermic prey**, such as frogs, lizards and snakes. Copperheads are specially adapted to give birth to live young instead of laying eggs, meaning they can live in cold places where most snakes can't survive. Scared snakes will hiss and throw their bodies around if threatened. They are dangerously **venomous**, although they prefer not to bite.

EASTERN GREY KANGAROO

Cluck, cluck – a mob of Eastern Greys talk to each other while they forage for grass, plants and fungi. You'll be able to spot this common 'big foot' almost everywhere across the eastern half of Australia. In the cooler parts of the day or in the evening they graze on the greenest grass because it contains more nutrients and is extra delicious.

Although these macropods can jump an astonishing six metres with a single hop, they are still victims of car accidents, so take care on roads at dawn and dusk.

GRAMPIANS GREVILLEA

When spring has sprung and the sun warms the cool earth beneath your feet, Grampians Grevillea display their beautiful pink clusters of flowers. These important plants make fabulous homes for insects and are a favourite delicacy for birds with brush-like tongues, such as lorikeets and honeyeaters.

GANG-GANG COCKATOO

Who's got the coolest red mohawk 'featherstyle' in the bush? It's the Gang-gang Cockatoo! Unlike other noisy members of their family, these cockatoos are usually pretty quiet, so you'll need to listen for seeds and nuts falling from trees to spot them. Occasionally you might hear their unusual call, which sounds like a creaky gate. These clever cockies choose a hollow to nest in, then chew the edges to make a soft bed for their eggs.

EASTERN PYGMY POSSUM

With a tiny pink nose, big pointed ears and soft whiskers, this little fella only weighs up to 40 grams – about the weight of a slice of bread! These teeny weeny possums love to eat nectar and pollen, so watch out for them near flowering gum trees and plants with flowers that look like brushes.

SHORT-BEAKED ECHIDNA

Spiky and slow, scratching around in the undergrowth, echidna snack on ants, termites and worms. Their spines are made of the same material as hair and they use smell and special electrical signals in their snouts to find food that they snap up with a long tongue.

When the males are ready to make babies, they follow the females around, and there can be up to ten in a line – an echidna train! Echidna and their relative the Platypus are the only animals in the world in the **monotreme** family. Out of their eggs hatch tiny babies called 'puggles'. Be careful on the roads – these slow waddlers don't know how to cross!

ACTIVITIES

LEAF HUNT

Go on a walk and see how many leaves you can find that match the pictures here. Draw the ones you've found inside the white box.

TREE FERN

VICTORIAN
CHRISTMAS BUSH

SILVER
BANKSIA

CASUARINA

GRAMPIANS
GREVILLEA

A-MAZE-ING

Help the pygmy possum to find some yummy treats in the darkness. There are three ways to solve this maze, can you complete them all?

RANGER'S TIP

Join the Junior Ranger program to learn more about the species that live here and how to interact with this special place.

"I am always grateful for the mountain views, the bird life and the big, tall trees".
Ranger Han

WORD PLAY

MANY LANGUAGES AROUND THE WORLD USE ONE WORD TO DESCRIBE A WHOLE FEELING OR EXPERIENCE.

SWEDISH – GÖKOTTA – GET UP EARLY AND GO OUTSIDE TO LISTEN TO THE BIRDS
JAPANESE – KOMOREBI – SUNLIGHT FLICKERING THROUGH THE LEAVES
FRENCH – DEPAYSEMENT – ALL THE FEELINGS YOU FEEL WHEN YOU'RE AWAY FROM HOME IN A NEW PLACE

CREATE YOUR OWN WORD TO DESCRIBE AN EXPERIENCE YOU'VE HAD HERE.

BUDJ BIM
NATIONAL PARK

There's nowhere else like Budj Bim in the country; here
you'll find crater lakes, lava canals, caves, stone huts
and one of the oldest aquaculture systems in the world.
You are standing on World Heritage Listed country that
changed our understanding of ancient science forever.
Become a part of the landscape as you learn about the
incredible things that happened here.

BUDJ BIM NATIONAL PARK
ID CARD

PARK ESTABLISHED: 1960
KNOWN FOR: CULTURAL HISTORY OF INTERNATIONAL IMPORTANCE
SIZE: 54.7 KM²
MEETING PLACE OF: GUNDITJMARA PEOPLE
GEOGRAPHY: VOLCANIC CRATERS AND CAVES WEAVING THROUGH WATERY FOREST

LITTLE EXPLORER'S GUIDE

MANNA GUM

With seed pods that branch out like a cross, white flowers and bark that falls off in long ribbons, Manna Gums are iconic to the Australian bush. This species is a true strong hero, with deep roots that lap at the groundwater and hold soil safely in position. They also provide a home and food to Koalas, possums, gliders, insects and birds. Their sweet sap can even be eaten by humans.

COMMON BRUSH-TAILED POSSUM

Resting in tree hollows during the day and dashing out at night for some **nocturnal** fun, 'brushies' might cause a commotion at your campsite as they bang, crash and scamper over human items. Their brush tail, cute pink nose and confident attitude make them pretty likeable, but human food makes them sick, so don't share your treats – they're better off eating leaves, flowers and fruits.

WESTERN GREY KANGAROO

Through the dappled light you catch a glimpse of furry ears and balancing tails – the kangaroos of the west live here. Beginning life no bigger than a jellybean and weighing less than a gram, babies climb with great determination through a forest of mum's fur to reach the safety of the pouch. Even more amazingly, they can't open their eyes at this stage so they have to climb blind! For a year, joeys hide in pouches that provide them with warmth, safety and milk. Listen for soft clicks as these furry friends chat to each other.

A VOLCANIC PAST

Deep inside the Earth, the temperature is so hot that rocks turn into a thick, fiery substance called magma. Pressure builds and some magma blows out onto the surface, where we call it lava.

Around 30,000 years ago the ancestors of the Gunditjmara people saw the Budj Bim volcano erupt and its lava flow across the land, hardening as it cooled. The high sections became volcanic rock and the low sections turned to craters, canals and caves. Over time the Gunditjmara used the new landscape to their advantage and changed some of these waterways for fish farming, providing food all year round for their communities.

SULPHUR-CRESTED COCKATOO

Sqwuaaaaaaak... a stark white beauty with a crest the yellow of sulphur screeches through the sky, breaking the silence. These birds are voracious munchers; watch for seeds, fruits, leaves and twigs falling from the sky. Even when they're not hungry they'll bite off pieces of trees and plants for seemingly no good reason – scientists think it might be to keep their beak short and sharp.

ANCIENT AQUACULTURE

The eruption of the Budj Bim volcano created beautiful shallow and deep sections where water could pool. When the lava stopped flowing around 6,700 years ago, the ancestors of the Gunditjmara people noticed the fish and eels becoming stuck in the pools, which made them easy to catch. They altered the waterways until they had the perfect balance of straighter areas mixed with sharp corners to slow the water and trap the animals in. Some eels got stuck for so long that they had their babies here, and so began the first aquaculture system in the world.

WATER RAT

As big as a platypus with a strong tail to use as a rudder, webbed feet like a duck for paddling and special fur that repels water, this is one incredibly designed aquatic creature. Look for it in places where the reeds and grasses are thick around the edges of the water, as this is where they like to hide. Water Rats eat fish, insects, freshwater **crustaceans** and even sometimes plants and birds, and carry their food to their favourite rocky feasting spot. Look for the scraps they've left behind by the water's edge.

DWARF GALAXIAS

In still or gently flowing water, watch as greeny-orange fish pop up to snatch insects from the surface. No bigger than the size of your little finger, these galaxias only live in freshwater and have no scales, only skin! Although they lay up to 250 eggs at a time, these little swimmers have had much of their **habitat** destroyed, causing it to be fragmented, and now they have trouble moving from place to place.

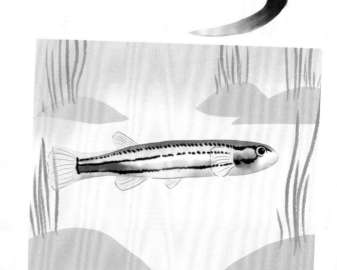

ACTIVITIES

"Once I head off on a walk into the park, I feel like I'm away from it all and nothing else matters. It's an amazing feeling to be wandering through the park with only the plant and animals for company."
Ranger Darren

WORD JUMBLE

Unjumble the aquaculture words below.

UNDAMARJTIG _____

HIFS _____

LEE _____

SLOPO _____

ANCVOLO _____

RANGER'S TIP

This ancient wonder is also the cultural home for the Gunditjmara people and the stone huts of their ancestors can still be found here. Show respect for culture and science by treading carefully and leaving everything where it is.

WATERPROOF OR NOT?

Use the table below to experiment with water. I wonder which surfaces you can find that repel water like the fur of a Water Rat?

MATERIAL	REPELS WATER	ATTRACTS WATER
E.g. Cotton	✗	✓

HIDDEN SECRETS *HIDE A POSSUM POUCH THEN DRAW YOUR FAMILY A MAP OR GIVE DIRECTIONS TO FIND IT. ONCE IT'S BEEN FOUND YOU CAN PLAY 'POSSUM' BY WEARING THE POUCH. I WONDER WHAT YOU'LL CARRY AROUND IN IT?*

Mount Buffalo
NATIONAL PARK

There is so much to see and do here, and you control the narrative. Climb up or down or all around, the cooler weather makes for perfect hiking temperatures. Alive with colour and wildlife, come and see the granite rocks as tall as buildings.

Feel the cold, clear water rush past your toes in the belly of a babbling brook or the splash of a waterfall cooling your arms, even the rush of wind across your face as you stare out into the great beyond. Which other feelings will capture your heart?

MOUNT BUFFALO NATIONAL PARK
ID CARD

PARK ESTABLISHED: 1898
KNOWN FOR: SNOWY-FACED WOMBATS AND COLOURFUL TREES
SIZE: 310км²
HOME OF: TAUNGURUNG PEOPLE
GEOGRAPHY: GRANITE MOUNTAINS CUT BY DEEP GORGES AND MAGNIFICENT WATERFALLS

LITTLE EXPLORER'S GUIDE

EASTERN RING-TAILED POSSUM

Bang, crash, rustle… these adorable acrobats swing, leap and hang with such skill, using their white-tipped tails as a third hand for grabbing. Not just a cute face, 'ring-tails' love a bit of teamwork. Mums and dads build special nests called 'dreys' together and the dads are the only male possums known to help the mums by carrying the babies while she eats in peace. To get a second go at the nutrients that already came out the other end, they often eat their own poo!

WOMBAT

Strong, robust and furry, these lovely waddling creatures make the perfect mountaineers. At sunset, wombats shuffle about to feed on whatever is available – leaves, grass, bark, moss and even fungi. Did you know that wombats use their strong claws for digging huge burrows 20 metres long and two metres deep? Even their pouches face backwards so that the babies don't get a face full of dirt!

Each wombat marks its territory with scent by rubbing up against things – logs and rocks will look 'polished' from so much rubbing. These weird and wonderful creatures have super-elastic intestines that create cube-shaped poo that won't roll off the side of the mountain. Poo also marks territory, so these wombats like to arrange their cubes in a stack – the higher the better.

ABORIGINAL GATHERINGS

Each summer for thousands of years, Aboriginal people from far and wide would travel to these mountains for important ceremonies for reasons such as celebrating big events and having important discussions. Some of the best bush tucker on the menu was Bogong moths that **migrate** here and rest in the rocks during the heat of the day. Smoke was used to encourage the moths out of their rocky hideaways and squishing them into a paste was a common way to eat them.

FLAME ROBIN

With a bright orange-red chest like a campfire, lookout for Flame Robins in clearings where they sit on low branches waiting to pounce on yummy **invertebrates**. Watch as they sprinkle lichen over their nests, ready to lay their blue and green eggs.

PIED CURRAWONG

Not a magpie and not a crow, these big black-and-white beauties eat lizards, berries, insects and smaller birds and sometimes hang their food up in the trees to save it for later. They make a stick bowl for a nest, but leave it high in the canopy so it's hard to see. Listen for their call that sounds like a wolf whistle or calling *currawong*, which is how they got their name.

SNOW GUM

Leaves droop and sway in the breeze as the Snow Gums use the cold snow and frost to develop their beautiful colours. Eucalypts are called 'sclerophyls', which means that they have hard leaves and can survive in harsh conditions. As they age, the trees get hit with wind, snow and ice, which causes them to twist. Look for thick, strong, twisty trees on your visit – which one do you guess is the oldest?

TAWNY FROGMOUTH

Everywhere around you are creatures great and small, this one so well **camouflaged** you may not notice it at all! Tawny feathers perfectly match the colours of the trees in which they **roost** and since they can stay perfectly still, they're hard to spot. They have special feathers with soft edges that make no sound as they hunt at night and sneak up on **prey**. Big eyes give frogmouths excellent night vision and they use their wide, yellow mouth to make a soft *oom oom* sound. Have you heard one yet?

ALPINE SILVER XENICA

A special butterfly that only lives here hangs out on the plateau around February and needs to fly while it's still warm enough to do so before winter arrives. Butterflies use their proboscis to eat nectar, but that's not how they taste it. Instead they work out if something is delicious or not by using taste receptors in their feet, and they can taste sweet, bitter, sour and salty!

ACTIVITIES

ACROSTIC FUN

Write an acrostic poem all about a cheeky wombat.

W --

O --

M --

B --

A --

T --

RANGER'S TIP

Pack carefully for your trip as the weather can change quickly and multiple times in a day. Prepared explorers will need warm clothing, a first aid kit, food, water and a map.

"The park makes me feel peaceful. I am in awe of its granite cliffs and views down to the valley. Mount Buffalo is sometimes called an island in the sky."
Ranger Zoey

SPOT THE DIFFERENCE

Circle the six differences between the Flame Robins.

AMAZING ACROBATS   ACROBATIC POSSUMS SWING FROM THE BRANCHES. HAVE A HANGING COMPETITION AND SEE WHO CAN HOLD ON THE LONGEST.

LITTLE DESERT
NATIONAL PARK

Plant your feet firmly on these vast, sandy plains speckled with mallee trees and wildflowers. It may look desolate at first glance; but take a closer look, have a listen and discover just who is hiding here in the littlest desert around.

By day, discover all the weird and wonderful plants and animals that have adapted to live here, by night sing songs by the campfire light and take your time to sit and think and just... be.

LITTLE DESERT NATIONAL PARK
ID CARD

PARK ESTABLISHED: 1968
KNOWN FOR: BIG SKIES AND STARRY NIGHTS
SIZE: 1,326KM²
HOME OF: WOTJOBALUK, JAADWA, JADAWADJALI, WERGAIA AND JUPAGULK PEOPLES (COLLECTIVELY WOTJOBALUK)
GEOGRAPHY: DESERT PLAINS

LITTLE EXPLORER'S GUIDE

LEAFLESS BITTER PEA

More than just yummy tucker, these bushes make a fabulous hiding place for tiny birds. The leaves are actually the tiny 'spikes' you can see along the stem; this shape helps them to save water in dry times. Their fruits are triangle-shaped pods with a single seed inside each – remarkable.

PAINTED DRAGON

'Painted' with a splash of yellow or orange around the neck and coated in a blue wash of colour, these friendly little lizards alter their colours to match their environment, becoming pale on white sand and darker on red sand.

Dragons are **ectothermic** so they must bask in the sun to gain energy and 'recharge', then zoom, watch them sprint to their burrows at the base of the saltbush plants. These guys eat ants all day long and you might even catch them communicating with others using arm waves, head bobs and tail swishes.

AUSTRALIAN PAINTED LADY

When the seasons change, these special butterflies **migrate** in large groups to follow the flowers across the landscape. Time is ticking because they only live for around 50 days. Butterflies are active during the day because they are **diurnal** and they use a long tube called a 'proboscis' to drink nectar. They land on different surfaces and collect minerals and moisture from their environment, even sweat from humans.

PEACOCK SPIDERS

An amazing thing about science is that we're always learning something new. Recently, citizen scientists sent in photos which caused entomologists to search in new places and actually discovered a new species here! Peacock spiders have eight legs, eight eyes and have a flap on their abdomen (like a fan) that is covered in amazing colours. They flip up the flap and do little dances to find a mate. They have spinnerets but don't build webs – they actually use them to vibrate their bodies in dances instead.

KREFFT'S GLIDER

Soft, tiny bodies float through the night sky, using their tails to steer as they glide from tree to tree. Krefft's Gliders live in groups called 'clans' and mark their 'spot' using scent glands on their chests. They have huge eyes for letting in extra light during the night when they emerge from hollows to feed on sweet nectar and fruits. In fact, we wouldn't have many of the forests we do if it weren't for animals like gliders spreading pollen as it falls off their fur as they glide down into the canopy.

RED-RUMPED PARROT

Look up to spot a flurry of feathers in blues and greens, with just a flash of red sitting on the lower back (rump). These parrots mate for life and rely on eucalypt hollows to build their nests. Mums sit on the eggs and dads feed them to keep them strong and healthy while they're working. You might see them near water or catch them eating seeds on the ground.

SATIN GREEN FORESTER

Fat brown caterpillars with patches of short hair that look like bumps hatch from bright yellow eggs and wriggle and munch all day until it's time to build a cocoon. After transforming on the inside – pop! – out comes a beautiful shimmering moth. You can identify females by the golden tip on the end of their abdomen, but it's important never to touch as it causes their beautiful scales to rub off and lose their colour. Insects are fragile, just like the environments in which they live.

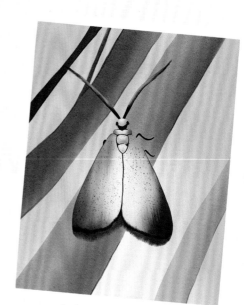

RUFOUS WHISTLER

The master of bush melodies, the Rufous Whistler is known for singing complicated songs and making noises that sound like whip cracks, whistles and trills. Look high up in the canopy to catch them flitting back and forth to catch insects or building cup-shaped nests stuck together with spider webs in the forks of trees.

LAUGHING KOOKABURRA

It may seem hilarious, but the laugh of a kookaburra is actually more like a yell to ask other birds to stay away – they're saying 'this is our spot'. When kookaburras catch something large like a lizard or a snake, you'll be able to see them whack it against the ground or a tree before eating it.

They make nests in tree hollows, but if there aren't any available they can fashion a little apartment out of a termite nest in the trees. They fly fast and crash into the mounds with their strong beaks. Doing this enough times creates a hole big enough for them to climb into and lay their eggs. When the babies hatch they eat some of the termites for nourishment and when the family no longer needs the nest, the birds fly away and the termites close the hole back over – clever.

ACTIVITIES

PAINT YOUR DRAGON

Design your own dragon pattern to help this lovely lizard attract a mate.

"Lost and at home all at the same time. It's magical to perch up on top of a sand dune and be surrounded by native plants and animals."
Ranger Andrew

RANGER'S TIP

Sometimes we can feel overwhelmed that the environmental issues of the world are too big for us to manage. If we all do one thing to help, we can all walk towards a healthy planet and a better future together.

WORD SEARCH

Test your knowledge of peacock spiders and find all the spidery words in the grid.

ENTOMOLOGIST
EIGHT LEGS
EIGHT EYES
FAN FLAP
ABDOMEN
PEACOCK
DANCE
SPINNERET
VIBRATE

E	X	D	K	L	Z	J	F	U	E	A	H	D	E	Q
I	I	N	F	W	I	A	I	T	Y	K	C	M	I	C
F	K	G	G	B	N	U	E	X	L	O	U	Q	G	T
W	B	Y	H	F	M	R	P	P	Y	G	B	V	H	E
K	U	F	L	T	E	M	L	S	V	N	P	A	T	E
W	C	A	I	N	L	M	L	W	I	W	B	G	E	C
U	P	O	N	U	B	E	E	K	R	I	X	H	Y	N
H	Q	I	C	B	I	U	G	X	K	J	J	K	E	A
M	P	O	Q	A	Y	D	S	S	O	R	M	N	S	D
S	W	L	C	R	E	V	I	B	R	A	T	E	P	R
B	U	B	N	E	P	P	R	T	Z	B	W	V	X	S
X	M	N	F	Y	T	T	W	N	E	M	O	D	B	A
J	H	P	V	X	B	E	K	G	Y	E	J	X	A	O
E	V	S	R	W	Z	O	M	H	Y	H	K	E	L	P
E	N	T	O	M	O	L	O	G	I	S	T	D	X	U

BUTTERFLY DANCING

DESIGN A DANCE TO SHOW THE LIFECYCLE OF A PAINTED LADY BUTTERFLY AS IT TRANSFORMS FROM EGG TO CATERPILLAR, THEN TO CHRYSALIS AND BUTTERFLY, BEFORE THE CYCLE BEGINS AGAIN. PERFORM IT TO YOUR FAMILY AND FRIENDS.

Murray Sunset
NATIONAL PARK

Out here it's so quiet that the breeze barely sends you a whisper as it tickles past your ear. This is a landscape that is forever moving and changing in the sun and rain and you might feel like you've landed on another planet.

In the daytime a whitewash of light bleaches sandy expanses hiding secretive animals that scurry from shelter to shelter. As the sun begins to dip, stand among the colour and feel yourself become a rainbow as the sunset illuminates the sky and the lakes in all shades of purple, orange, yellow and pink.

MURRAY SUNSET NATIONAL PARK
ID CARD

PARK ESTABLISHED: 1991
KNOWN FOR: PINK LAKES AND INCREDIBLE SUNSETS
SIZE: 6,330KM²
CULTURAL COUNTRY OF: LATJI LATJI, NGINTAIT AND NYERI NYERI PEOPLE
GEOGRAPHY: ARID PLAINS SCATTERED WITH ANCIENT TREES AND SALTY LAKES

REGENT PARROT

Among the mallee scrub, Regent Parrots munch on grass seeds on the ground. They use different calls for different needs – *carrack carrack* is for calling out, whereas *twitter twitter* is for chatting between mates. You might spot their long pointy tails poking out of nesting hollows in River Red Gums.

RED KANGAROO

Bounding across the plains with their powerful legs and tails at more than 50 kilometres per hour, the Red Kangaroo is the largest **marsupial** in the world. Males can weigh almost 100 kilograms and are taller than many adult humans.

These **herbivores** live in mobs across Australia in some of the driest places and get most of their water from the foods they eat. Look out for them grazing on the lakebed. Mother kangaroos have a special trick called 'embryonic diapause' – they can stop a baby from being born until the previous baby has left the pouch. No room for two when you're always on the move.

SUNSETS

As the Earth spins on its axis and completes its turn to end the day, we say goodbye sun and hello stars. Ablaze with colour, the wide-open sky burns pink, orange, yellow and purple in this desert paradise. Far away from pollution, clean air out here keeps colours bright and not muted. In the late afternoon the light takes a longer path to get to our eyes and scatters differently in the air – this changes the colours that we can see, giving us a sunset.

PINK COCKATOO

In the cooler parts of the day watch out for these pink crested beauties foraging on the ground for seeds and insects with their mates the Galahs and corellas. Watch closely as the first two come in to scout for danger, then call out to friends to let them know it's safe. Did you know that Pink Cockatoos are left- or right-footed, like we are left- or right-handed? Watch closely to see who uses which.

MURRAY LILY

This plant loves wetlands so much, it's listed as an 'indicator species' to help scientists to know whether an area should be listed as a wetland or not. From a bulb in the ground grow clumps of leaves, topped with huge white flowers. The bulbs were important food for the traditional owners of this country.

PINK LAKES

You're looking at an optical illusion. The water here is actually clear, but beneath the surface the lakebed is made of hard salt and this is a perfect place for special salt-loving algae to grow. The algae makes 'carotenoids' that are red or pink and these help it to photosynthesise and grow. The colour of the carotenoids makes the lakes look pink! The lakes change colour throughout the day – I wonder how many colours you can count?

MALLEEFOWL

These megapodes use their big feet to build mounds of sand and leaves where they lay their eggs. Some can be four metres wide – the size of your bedroom! The males do all the nest building and make sure to leave a hole in the top for the eggs to fall in. Once the eggs are in, they cover them over with leaves. As the leaves break down, they produce warmth that keeps the eggs warm – the same as the vegetables breaking down in your compost at home. Dad Malleefowl work hard to keep the nest temperature at 33 degrees and spend all day adding more leaves or taking some away to get it just right.

GILES' PLANIGALE

In winter you might just catch this triangle-headed, short-legged **carnivore** basking in the sun to save energy. Also known as Paucident Planigales, they love a crunchy diet of spiders, cockroaches and beetles. Because they live in very hot places, they use plants and cracks in the soil as shelter during the heat of the day.

CENTRAL BEARDED DRAGON

Head out early in the morning to spy 'beardies' flattening their bodies on rocks and logs to capture more heat for movement. The spiky scales under their chins look like a beard and they almost seem like a tiny version of a mythical dragon from your storybooks. Their colours are just like the earth, rocks and leaves around them and in just a few minutes they can change colour to match their space.

They communicate with animal sign language – bobbing heads to show strength to other males and waving arms to say that they admit defeat and would like to be friends. Survival is thirsty work, so when it rains they angle their bodies up to face the sky, open their mouths and let the rain fall straight in!

YELLOW-FACED WHIPSNAKE

Slim and sleek, these whipsnakes sport a fancy flick of black from their eye to the corner of their mouth and their tail tapers down to a pointy tip. They love eating lizards and the eggs of other animals and can lay up to 20 of their own. Sometimes if a really good spot is found to protect their eggs, lots of snakes will lay their eggs in the same pile – hundreds from different parents all nestled away in their little snake nursery.

ACTIVITIES

NATURE SUDOKU

Complete the sudoku puzzle by drawing in the missing icons. Each image must appear only once in each row, column and grid.

RANGER'S TIP

Remote parks can have patchy phone signal. Make sure you download maps to use offline and installing an emergency app on your devices can be useful in the rare event that you need to call for help.

COMPASS ADVENTURE

Pretend you're a Red Kangaroo and bounce your way around the pink lake to a shady resting place. Start at the arrow and follow the dots according to the directions.

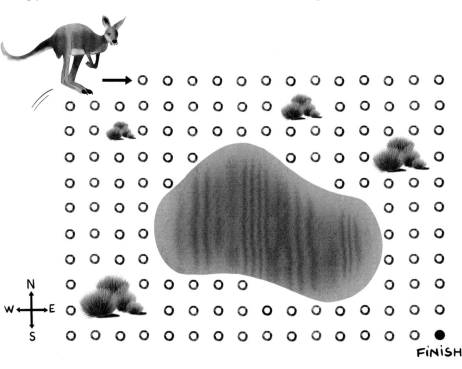

FINISH

DIRECTIONS

MOVE 3 DOTS EAST
MOVE 2 DOTS SOUTH
MOVE 6 DOTS EAST
MOVE 2 DOTS NORTH
MOVE 4 DOTS EAST
MOVE 10 DOTS SOUTH

CHATTERBOX FACTS — *MAKE A CHATTERBOX USING THE ANIMALS FROM THIS CHAPTER. FLIP THE SECTION TO READ OUT SOME FUN FACTS ABOUT THE ANIMAL TO YOUR FRIENDS OR FAMILY.*

FINAL QUIZ

Now that you've finished your reading and exploring, here's one last quiz to check what you learned. Check back through the book for the answers.

1 What does the algae make in salty lakes to make the colour appear pink?

2 Animal poo is called ...

3 How fast can a Peregrine Falcon dive?

4 How do tree ferns protect themselves from fire?

5 How can you tell male and female Galah apart?

6 What does a Scarlet Honeyeater sound like?

7 List two venomous animals from the book.

8 Butterflies build a _ _ _ _ _ _ _ _ _ and moths build a _ _ _ _ _ _ in order to pupate.

9 Why do kookaburras laugh?

10 Why do wombats 'polish' logs and rocks?

Answers on inside back cover.

KEYWORDS EXPLAINED

Amphibian	Cold-blooded animals with a backbone that can breathe underwater at a stage of their life.
Camouflage	When animals and plants match their colours to their surroundings to blend in and hide from predators.
Carnivore	Eats only meat.
Crustacean	Animals that usually live in water and have a hard shell, segmented body and joints.
Diurnal	Animals that are active during the day.
Ecologist	A scientist who studies animals, plants, air and water.
Ecosystem	A community of living things in their natural environment.
Extinct	When all the animals and plants of a particular species have died out.
Fauna	Animals.
Flora	Plants.
Habitat	The place where animals and plants live and gain everything they require to survive.
Herbivore	Eats only plant matter.
Invertebrate	Animals without backbones.
Mammal	Warm-blooded animals that produce milk.
Marsupial	Mammals that have pouches.
Migrate	When animals temporarily move from one area to another in search of food, a mate or better weather.
Nocturnal	Animals that sleep during the day and hunt or forage at night.
Omnivore	Eats both meat and plant matter.
Predator	An animal or plant that eats other animals or plants.
Prey	An animal or plant that gets eaten by other animals or plants.
Reptile	Cold-blooded animals with a backbone that have scaly skin.
Roost	When animals rest or sleep up high in trees or other structures.
Scat	Animal poo.
Sediment	Tiny particles of soil in water that eventually settle to the bottom.
Venomous	An animal that injects or secretes a dangerous substance into its prey, or animals that pose a threat.

PLEDGE TO THE PLANET

Now you know all about Victorian national parks and how to make better choices to protect plants, animals and culture, you can show your commitment by saying the pledge.

Have an adult record you speaking the pledge and signing it.

As a child of the world and a responsible citizen of our community,
I pledge to do what I can at home, at school and in my community,
To use less stuff,
Find new ways to do things,
Get outside more often,
Keep my distance from wild animals,
Respect and celebrate the culture of the places I visit,
Tell people about the amazing things I've learnt about nature; and
Do the right thing even when nobody is looking.
I love my planet and we can all work together to keep it healthy for our future.

Signed . . . .

FIND OUT MORE

For keen little scientists wanting to read more about the fascinating animals, plants and culture detailed in this book, you can read on here:

Australian Geographic
Australian Marine Conservation
  Society
Australian Museum
Australians Together

Birdlife Australia
Bush Heritage Australia
Cool Australia
Marine Conservation Institute
Museums Victoria

Parks Victoria
The Nature Conservancy
United Nations Educational, Scientific
  and Cultural Organisation
  (UNESCO)

Victorian Department of
  Sustainability and Environment
Wildlife Information Rescue and
  Education Service (WIRES)
World Wildlife Fund (WWF)

Published in 2024 by Reed New Holland Publishers
Sydney

Level 1, 178 Fox Valley Road, Wahroonga, NSW 2076, Australia

newhollandpublishers.com

Copyright © 2024 Reed New Holland Publishers
Copyright © 2024 in text: Chloe Butterfield
Copyright © 2024 in illustrations: Deborah Bianchetto

Printed in China

10 9 8 7 6 5 4 3 2 1

A record of this book is held at the National Library of Australia.

ISBN 978 1 76079 616 7

Managing Director: Fiona Schultz
Publisher and Project Editor: Simon Papps
Designer: Andrew Davies
Production Director: Arlene Gippert

OTHER TITLES BY REED NEW HOLLAND INCLUDE:

Little Explorer's Guide to Australian National Parks ISBN 978 1 76079 615 0
Little Explorer's Guide to New South Wales National Parks ISBN 978 1 92107 315 1
Little Explorer's Guide to Queensland National Parks ISBN 978 1 76079 521 4
Chris Humfrey's Awesome Australian Animals ISBN 978 1 92554 670 5
Chris Humfrey's Coolest Creepy Crawlies ISBN 978 1 76079 445 3
Chris Humfrey's Incredible Coastal Critters ISBN 978 1 76079 446 0

For details of hundreds of other Natural History titles see newhollandpublishers.com

And keep up with Reed New Holland and New Holland Publishers on Facebook and Instagram

 ReedNewHolland and NewHollandPublishers
 @ReedNewHolland and @NewHollandPublishers